Wilf and Wilma went to a dolphin pool.

The dolphins played with the ball.

Wilma climbed up the ladder.

A dolphin jumped through the hoop.

Wilf gave the dolphin some fish.

Wilma gave the dolphin some fish.

They looked at the killer-whale.

The killer-whale was big.

The killer-whale looked at Wilf.

Wilma gave it some fish.

The killer-whale jumped up.

It took the fish.

The killer-whale went splash.

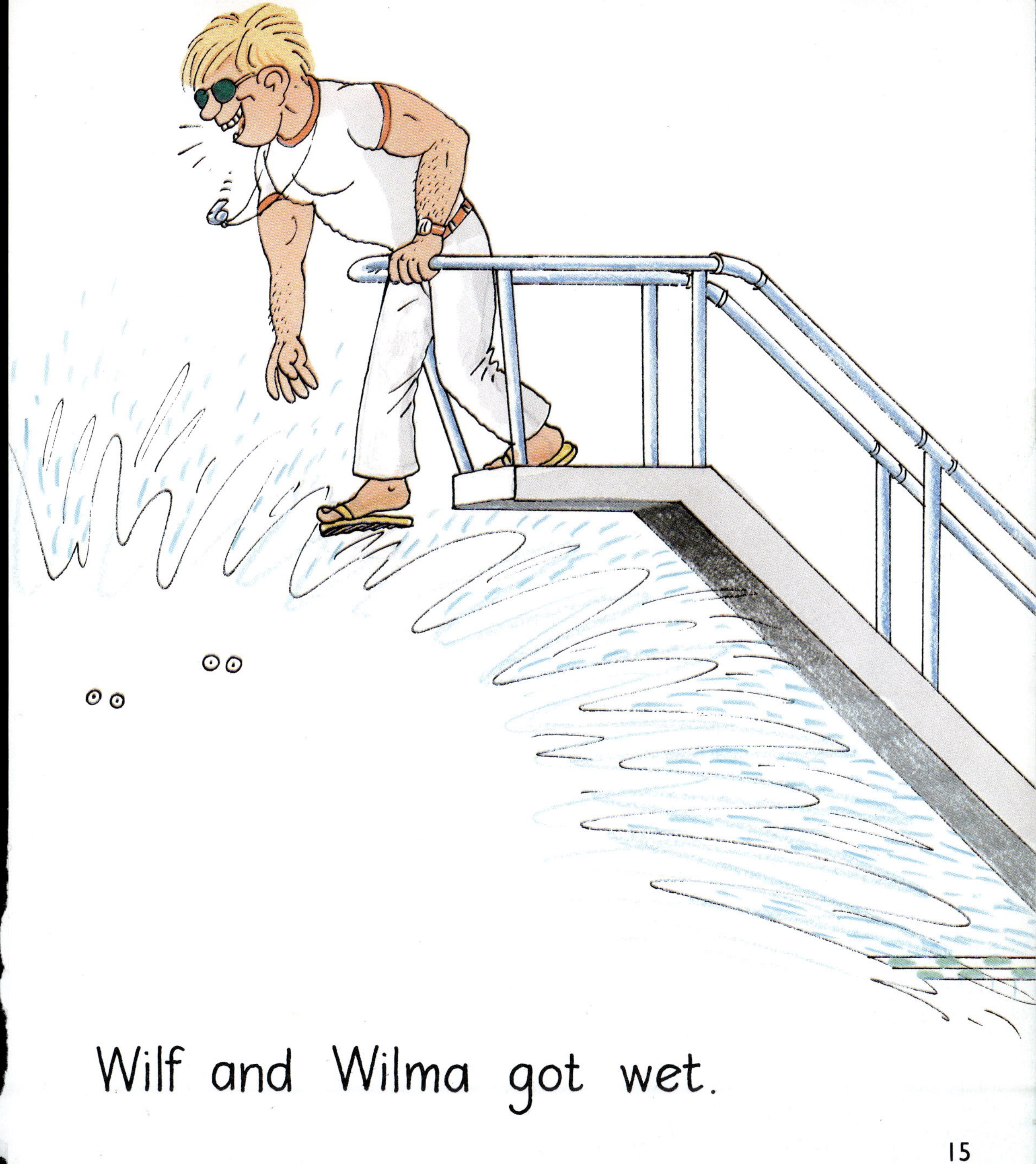

Wilf and Wilma got wet.

'Oh no!' said Wilf.
'Oh no!' said Wilma.